STEM Projects in **MINECRAFT®**

The Unofficial Guide to MINECRAFT® Environments

JILL KEPPELER

PowerKiDS press

Published in 2025 by The Rosen Publishing Group, Inc.
2544 Clinton Street, Buffalo, NY 14224

First Edition

Editor: Greg Roza
Book Design: Rachel Rising
Illustrator: Matias Lapegüe

Photo Credits: Cover, pp. 1, 3–24 Soloma/Shutterstock.com; p. 4, 6, 8, 10, 12, 14, 16, 18 Levent Konuk/Shutterstock.com; p. 5 Urda Cristian/Shutterstock.com; p. 17 JoannaPerchaluk/Shutterstock.com; p. 20 Pixel-Shot/Shutterstock.com; p. 21 JanBussan/Shutterstock.com.

Library of Congress Cataloging-in-Publication Data

Names: Keppeler, Jill, author.
Title: The unofficial guide to Minecraft environments / Jill Keppeler.
Description: New York : PowerKids Press, [2025] | Series: STEM Projects in Minecraft | Includes index.
Identifiers: LCCN 2023057062 (print) | LCCN 2023057063 (ebook) | ISBN 9781499446968 (library binding) | ISBN 9781499446951 (paperback) | ISBN 9781499446975 (ebook)
Subjects: LCSH: Minecraft (Game)–Handbooks, manuals, etc.–Juvenile literature. | Biotic communities–Computer simulation–Juvenile literature. | Ecology–Experiments–Juvenile literature. | Habitat (Ecology)–Juvenile literature. | Habitat conservation–Juvenile literature. | Science projects–Juvenile literature.
Classification: LCC GV1469.35.M535 K459 2025 (print) | LCC GV1469.35.M535 (ebook) | DDC 794.8/5–dc23/eng/20240105
LC record available at https://lccn.loc.gov/2023057062
LC ebook record available at https://lccn.loc.gov/2023057063

Manufactured in the United States of America

CPSIA Compliance Information: Batch #CSPK25. For further information contact Rosen Publishing at 1-800-237-9932.

Contents

Biomes and Environments

Every *Minecraft* world, just like the real world, has a vast combination of environments or biomes. These are natural communities of plants and animals. Biomes in *Minecraft* may have different life-forms or mobs, trees and plants, types of earth, weather, and water or grass colors. Most (but not all) have matching counterparts in the real world.

Even within biome categories, or groups, there are differences. Knowing these groups and differences can help you find **resources** in the game—and help you better understand the natural world you live in. It's just one more way you can learn about STEM topics by exploring *Minecraft* environments.

MINECRAFT MANIA

Woodland mansions, or large houses, only spawn, or appear, in *Minecraft* dark forest biomes. So, it's important to be able to know what this biome looks like if you want to find a mansion!

Some forests can be dark in the real world because many big trees keep light from reaching the ground. It's the same in *Minecraft*!

A List of Lands

While there are dozens of kinds of *Minecraft* biomes, these kinds can fit in a handful of basic groups. In fact, they can be grouped in several different ways, and this book will look at a few of those. For example, all ocean biomes have similarities, but they can have different climates. A warm ocean biome is very different from a frozen ocean one!

Environments generally can be put in forest, cave, mountain and hill, ocean, swamp, plains, and desert/badlands groups. There are also biomes in other **dimensions** that don't have any real-world matches, such as the End and the Nether biomes.

MINECRAFT MANIA

Mushroom islands are a unique, or one of a kind, biome. These rare islands have giant mushrooms, and the only mobs are mooshrooms, which are like red mushroom cows.

Like a desert, a badlands biome has lots of sand, little water, and some cacti and dead bushes. However, it has red sand instead of regular sand and lots of terracotta, or baked clay.

You can probably guess the basics of the biome groups. Forests have lots of plants and trees, so there are lots of resources. Caves are underground. Mountainous biomes have lots of higher **terrain** that can be rocky or snow covered, while plains are mostly flat and much closer to sea level.

Swamps are also flat and low, with a lot of shallow water covering the land. Deserts and mesas (or badlands) have a lot of sand, few plants, and no rain or snow. Ocean biomes are just that—huge spans of deep water! There are real-world **versions** of all these biomes.

MINECRAFT MANIA

In *Minecraft*, the height of the regular world is about 320 blocks. Natural terrain can go up to about 255 blocks. Clouds drift by at about 190 blocks high. Sea level is about 62 blocks.

Some swamps are mangrove swamps. They have mangrove trees, which have roots outside the earth and only grow in that biome.

Weather Ways

Minecraft's environments have a few different markers for climate. One is temperature, or how hot or cold the environment usually is. This affects if there's ice or snow on the ground. It also affects the second marker: **precipitation**. Colder biomes will get snow instead of rain, and the snow can pile up. Even some milder biomes can get snow above a certain height.

During rain or snowfall, the sky can get very dark. It gets especially dark during thunderstorms. These may also have lightning, which can start fires and damage, or hurt, mobs—and players!

MINECRAFT MANIA

Powder snow can be a danger in some *Minecraft* biomes. Players can fall through powder snow and take freezing damage while stuck in it! To avoid this, wear leather boots while traveling through snow.

Different biomes may have different types of villages and villagers. Buildings will be made of different materials, such as this house made of acacia wood in a **savanna** biome.

Plant Life

Within the basic *Minecraft* environment groups, there's a lot of **variety**. One way you can see that is with the biomes' plants. *Minecraft* jungles, **taigas**, dark forests, and flower forests are all forests, but they have different types of trees and other plants. Cherry groves are mountainous biomes because they only **generate** at a certain height, but they're also the only place you can find cherry trees.

Knowing your *Minecraft* plants can help you figure out what kind of a biome you're in. If you see dark oak trees, you're in a dark forest biome. That's the only place they grow!

MINECRAFT MANIA

Sunflowers, which always face east, only grow in sunflower plains biomes. If you see cacti, you're in a desert or badlands environment.

Three kinds of trees can be bigger around than other *Minecraft* trees. Dark oak (shown), jungle, and spruce trees may all be two blocks by two blocks wide. Dark oaks can be up to eight blocks tall, but jungle and spruce trees can be much taller!

dark oak tree

cherry tree

Plants can help you figure out ocean or cave biomes too. Seagrass grows on the floor of every ocean environment except for frozen oceans. Kelp grows in oceans except for warm or frozen types. In cave biomes, there can be huge differences with plants. Lush caves have unique plants including moss, cave vines, and dripleaf plants.

Grass, grass blocks, and sometimes tree leaves will be different colors in different biomes. (As can water.) Drier environments (deserts, badlands, savannas) have more brownish colors, and swamps have a dark olive-green color. Grass in jungles is bright green, and taigas have blue-green grass.

MINECRAFT MANIA

Other *Minecraft* cave biomes include dripstone caves and deep dark caves. Deep dark caves generate very deep underground and may have **ancient** cities in them!

Minecraft (and real-world) corals aren't plants; they're tiny ocean creatures that live in groups. Coral reefs only appear in *Minecraft* warm ocean biomes.

Many Mobs

Many *Minecraft* mobs only spawn in certain biomes, and some mobs only spawn in certain places within those biomes. For example, camels will only appear in desert villages. Axolotls spawn in lush caves, while turtles spawn on beaches. Pandas appear only in jungles and are more common in bamboo-type jungles.

Some mobs have different types depending on where they spawn. Rabbits are yellow when they spawn in deserts, white or black and white in snowy or frozen biomes, or black or brown in some forests and meadows. With frogs, their color can depend on where they grew up!

MINECRAFT MANIA

Minecraft has passive, neutral, and hostile mobs. Passive mobs, such as cows, will not attack players. Neutral mobs, such as bees, will attack in some cases. Hostile mobs, such as zombies, will always attack!

Minecraft foxes usually spawn in taigas. They will be white when they spawn in snowy taigas, but reddish in other biomes. Real-world Arctic foxes will be white in winter and red, brown, or gray in summer!

Different Dimensions

The Nether and the End are different dimensions in *Minecraft*. They each have their own biomes that have blocks, items, and mobs that you can't find anywhere else. The End's main island is where players can fight the ender dragon. There are many smaller islands in the distance around it. Other than the dragon, only endermen and shulkers spawn there.

The Nether has a greater variety. Its biomes have mobs including ghasts, magma cubes, piglins, and wither skeletons in various places. Unique buildings include nether fortresses and bastion remnants. It's the only place to find soul sand, netherrack, unique **fungi**, and many other resources.

MINECRAFT MANIA

Crimson forests have hoglins (hostile mobs that look like pigs) and piglins that hunt the hoglins for the pork chops that they'll drop. This makes it one of the few biomes with a food chain!

Blazes are fiery mobs that only spawn in Nether fortresses. They're the only source of blaze rods.

Finding Your Way

You can see how understanding environments in *Minecraft* can help you when playing the game. Each biome has unique mobs, plants, and other resources for you to find. For example, do you remember where woodland mansions spawn after reading this book? What sort of trees do you need to look for?

The real world may not have haunted woodland mansions, but it does have biomes! Each type of biome has its own kinds of animals and plants that have adapted to live in its particular conditions and climate. Understanding how *Minecraft* environments work can also help you understand the world we live in.

This photo shows a biome full of birch trees. *Minecraft* also has birch forests! The trees have the same white bark.

Glossary

ancient: Very old.

dimension: A level of existence.

fungus: A living thing that's like a plant but that doesn't have leaves, flowers, or green color or make its own food. The plural form is fungi.

generate: To cause to be created.

precipitation: Water that falls to the ground as hail, mist, rain, sleet, or snow.

resource: Something that can be used.

savanna: A grassland with scattered patches of trees.

taiga: A biome that includes a humid, cold forest environment with many spruce or fir trees.

terrain: A type of land in an area.

variety: The state of having many different things.

version: A form of something that is different from others.

For More Information

BOOKS

Latham, Donna. *Biomes: Discover the Earth's Ecosystems*. White River Junction, VT: Nomad Press, 2019.

Mojang AB and the Official Minecraft Team. *Minecraft Guide to Survival*. New York, NY: Random House Worlds, 2022.

WEBSITES

Biomes
www.ign.com/wikis/minecraft/Biomes
The IGN site provides more information on biomes in *Minecraft*.

Habitats
kids.nationalgeographic.com/nature/habitats
National Geographic Kids takes a look at the natural environments of plants and animals.

World Biomes and Ecosystems
www.ducksters.com/science/ecosystems/world_biomes.php
Ducksters looks into the types of biomes on Earth.

Index